TRAVEL GAMES
FOR THE FAMILY

Marie Boatness

Illustrations by Mark L. Woodruff

Manufactured in the United States of America.

This edition published by Canyon Creek Press, 5714 E. Dale Lane, Cave Creek, Arizona 85331; 602-585-3059

10   9   8   7   6   5   4   3   2   1

Publisher's **Cataloging in Publication Data**

Boatness, Marie

794
BOA

   Travel games for the family/ by Marie Boatness

ISBN 0-9635619-0-1

LC 93-90005   794

   1. Games for travelers—Juvenile literature. 2. Games. 3. Travel—games. I. Title.

DEDICATION

This book is dedicated to Paul and Tara, who inspired me to write these games as we traveled on our many trips. Also, to Ron, my husband, who continually encouraged and improved my ideas.

ACKNOWLEDGMENT

To Mary Westheimer who edited this book and became my chief consultant.

INTRODUCTION

This book offers the entire family hours of entertainment. The rules are easy and the games are fun—and challenging to the imagination.

Scoring is strictly optional. If your family wishes to have the games less competitive, simply omit the scores.

SUPPLIES NEEDED

Although most of the supplies you will need for the games in this book can be picked up along the way, you might want to start out with these materials:

- Pencils or pens for each player
- Tablet of paper
- Piece of cardboard
- Crayons (optional)
- Discarded newspaper and magazines
- Watch with a second hand
- Several plastic spoons
- Five pennies (or any coin) for each of two players
- Straws
- Several paper bags
- Scissors (optional)
- Flashlight
- Bag of marshmallows, small box of raisins and toothpicks
- Road maps of the trip

TABLE OF CONTENTS

ACTION GAMES

MAZES

No. of Players: unlimited
Age: 8 to adult
Supplies: paper and pencil for each player and a watch or clock
Location: anywhere

Use a pencil to create mazes and then exchange papers. Time the players to see how fast the maze can be completed.

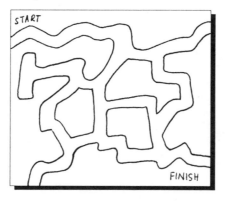

THIS IS MY FOOT

No. of Players: unlimited
Age: all
Supplies: none
Location: anywhere

One player is **It**. That player touches his or her foot and says, "This is my **nose**." The next player touches his or her own nose and says, "This is my **ear**." The next player touches his or her own ear and says, "This is my **elbow**." The game continues until one player is tricked into actually saying the part of the body that person is touching. Each player has 10 seconds to complete his or her turn.

Scoring: Everyone starts with five points. Take away one point for a miss, and the player with the most points after 10 rounds wins.

TEAR IT LONG

No. of Players: unlimited
Age: all
Supplies: a discarded newspaper and a watch or clock
Location: anywhere

Each player gets a piece of paper or newspaper equal in size. Each then tries to tear the longest continuous piece of paper without tearing it in two. Tearing in a circular fashion is one way to make one long piece of paper. Time the players.

Scoring: The person with the longest piece in one minute wins.

TIME ME

No. of Players:	unlimited
Age:	all
Supplies:	a watch or clock
Location:	anywhere

Pick an easy activity, such as taking off and putting on a shoe, and time each other to see who can perform the skill the fastest.

Other timeable skills include:

- ◆ socks on and off
- ◆ jacket on and off
- ◆ piece or pieces of jewelry on and off
- ◆ combination of above.

CALL IT

No. of Players:	unlimited in groups of two
Age:	all
Supplies:	none
Location:	anywhere

Players pair off in groups of two. Each player hides one hand behind his or her back. On the signal "one, two, three, show" (from a nonplayer), all of the players bring their hidden hands forward, showing a certain number of fingers. A fist equals zero.

At the same time the hands come forward, the players guess out loud how many fingers the opponent will show. If someone thinks a fist will be shown, they say, "Zero."

Scoring: Players get one point each time they guess the correct number of fingers displayed by their opponent.

I'M COORDINATED

No. of Players:	unlimited
Age:	all
Supplies:	none
Location:	anywhere

Everyone tries to rub their tummies and pat their heads at the same time.

Variations: They then try to do the above but switch hands. Next they rub a partner's tummy and head.

This game gets everybody giggling.

I'M SUPER COORDINATED

No. of Players: unlimited
Age: 7 to adult
Supplies: none
Location: anywhere

Players take turns being the leader. The leader calls out the following signals:

1. "Write the number one in the air with your right index finger and write the number two in the air with your left index finger.

2. "Now do these at the same time."

3. "Write the number one in the air with your left index finger and write the number two in the air with your right index finger.

4. "Now do these at the same time."

Variation: This game can go to the number 10 and any combination of numbers can be used.

PUZZLE TIME

No. of Players:	two
Age:	7 to adult
Supplies:	one piece of paper, a pencil and a watch or clock
Location:	anywhere

Take a piece of paper and draw five to 10 zigzag lines on the paper. Now carefully cut or tear the pieces and give them to another player. Time that person to see how quickly he or she can put the puzzle together.

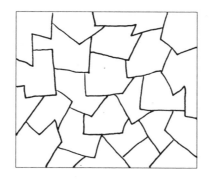

HUMAN, NET, BUTTERFLY

No. of Players: unlimited
Age: all
Supplies: none
Location: anywhere

All of the players count to three. On the number three, each person makes one of the following signals:

- ◆ human (pretend to look through binoculars by making two circles with the thumbs and index fingers)

- ◆ butterfly net (make a big circle overhead with the

fingertips touching)

◆ butterfly (extend forearms out to the side like wings).

Scoring: Human beats the net, net beats the butterfly, butterfly beats the human. Score one point for each signal which beats another. Ten points wins the game.

AUTO BASKETBALL

No. of Players: two
Age: all
Supplies: wadded pieces of paper
Location: anywhere

One person makes a basket with his or her arms and the other players shoot baskets with wadded pieces of paper. The basket can be made smaller or larger and the distances closer or farther depending upon the skill or desire of the players.

Variation: A cup can also be used at various distances instead of arms.

Scoring: Score two points for each basket and three points for long distance shots.

JOUSTING SPOONS

No. of Players: two
Age: all
Supplies: two spoons and two wadded pieces of paper
Location: anywhere

Each player takes a plastic spoon and places a wadded piece of paper on it. On the word "go," each person uses the spoon to try and knock the other player's paper off.

Scoring: The first to succeed wins a point. Ten points wins the game.

PENNY ARCADE

No. of Players: unlimited
Age: all
Supplies: a magazine or piece of cardboard, and two pennies (or any coin)
Location: anywhere

Draw a line down the middle of the magazine or piece of cardboard to make your board. Place penny A on one side of the board and penny B on the edge of the opposite end of the board.

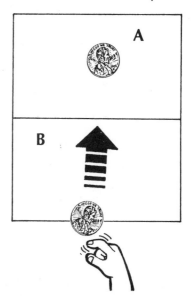

Each player now takes a turn shooting penny B by flicking the thumb and forefinger at penny B, trying to knock A off the board.

Scoring: One point for each penny hit off the board. Ten points wins the game.

Variation: Put five or more pennies on the board and shoot at all of them.

ON THE EDGE

No. of Players: unlimited
Age: all
Supplies: a magazine or piece of cardboard, and a penny
Location: anywhere

One player places a penny at the edge of the board, and everyone takes turns flicking the penny to the opposite side of the cardboard with their forefingers. Players try to see who can shoot the penny closest to the opposite side of the cardboard without shooting it off.

Scoring: Score one point for being closest to the edge. Ten points wins the game.

Variation: Use a straw to blow a wadded piece of paper to the edge of the board.

BOARD SOCCER

No. of Players: two
Age: all
Supplies: a magazine or piece of cardboard, two straws and a wadded piece of paper
Location: anywhere

The players sit with the board between them and attempt to blow a wadded piece of paper off the opponent's side of the board using their own straws. No one can touch the wadded paper.

Scoring: Score one point each time the paper is blown off the opponent's side.

ADD A MOTION

No. of Players:	unlimited
Age:	all
Supplies:	none
Location:	anywhere

One person starts the game by doing one motion, such as waving a hand.

The next person does that motion and then adds a motion. For instance, the player might wave a hand then nod his head.

This goes on with each player taking a turn, doing all of the motions previously shown and then adding a motion. The person who forgets a motion loses a point.

Scoring: Any player who loses five points is out of the game until the next round.

ALPHABET GAMES

SPELL AND BEEP

No. of Players: unlimited
Age: 7 to adult
Supplies: none
Location: anywhere

One player picks a word and then each person takes a turn saying one letter of the alphabet. For example, if the word is "tree," the first person says the first letter of the alphabet, "A." The next person says, "B" and on through the alphabet until any letter in the word "tree" comes up. When the letter "E" comes up, the person who is next says, "Beep" instead of "E."

The players who have a turn at the letters "T" and "R" must also say "beep" in place of the letters.

Scoring: Anyone who forgets to say "beep" has one point scored **against** him or her. Five points eliminates a player from the game.

THE ALPHABET GAME

No. of Players: unlimited
Age: all
Supplies: a watch or clock (optional)
Location: a view of the outdoors

All of the players start with the letter "A" and one at a time name out loud an object they see (or have seen) inside or outside the vehicle that begins with that letter.

For example, one player starts with "A—animal." The next follows with "B—billboard," etc.

The game continues through the alphabet, with players dropping out as they are unable to come up with a word for their letter.

Variation: One person goes at a time and the fastest player through the alphabet wins. Someone must time each player, and no answer can be repeated.

SHOPPING BY THE LETTERS

No. of Players: unlimited
Age: 7 to adult
Supplies: none
Location: anywhere

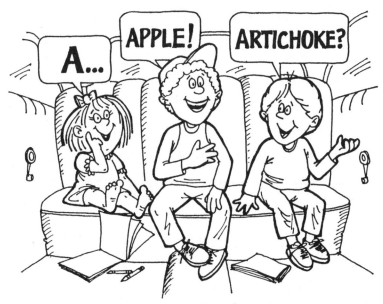

One person at a time says a letter. In turn, the rest of the players must name a food item they can find in the grocery store with that letter. Now the next person says a letter and the game continues. Players cannot repeat a letter.

Scoring: Score one point for each answer. Twenty points wins the game.

Variation: In place of a grocery store, use a hardware store, sporting goods store, etc.

WHERE'S YOUR NEXT STOP? WHAT WILL YOU SEE?

No. of Players:	unlimited
Age:	7 to adult
Supplies:	none
Location:	anywhere

One player asks, "Where's your next stop?" Another player must answer by choosing a word that begins with the letter "A," perhaps "Alaska." The player is then asked, "What will you see?" He or she must answer with another word that begins with an "A," such as "airplane."

Another player is asked the same two questions, but must answer by choosing a word that begins with the letter "B." The players continue through the alphabet. Any word that begins with the correct letter can be used as answers.

SPELL AND MOVE

No. of Players: unlimited
Age: 7 to adult
Supplies: none
Location: anywhere

A player is selected as the leader and designates chosen actions to replace certain letters of the alphabet. The leader than says a word, and another player spells the word, replacing the designated letters with the actions.

For example, the leader might say, "Clap on the letter 'A,' snap your fingers on the letter 'C,' and wiggle your fingers on the letter 'O.' "

If the word is "actor," the player claps (for "A"), snaps fingers (for "C"), says, "T," wiggles fingers (for "O") and says, "R."

Variation: Instead of performing actions, make sounds when spelling designated letters (say, "Oink" for "A," laugh for "D," etc.)

ART GAMES

DRAW THE TALE

No. of Players: unlimited
Age: all
Supplies: paper and pencil for each player
Location: anywhere

Any player begins to tell a short story (approximately 10 sentences) with one scene. As the scene is described, the other players draw it.

For example, "One rainy day a boy rode his bike home." All of the players draw a boy riding his bike home in the rain.

The first player continues, "Up came a big dog with long ears." The other players draw the dog into the same scene.

When the story is over, everyone compares pictures. The differences will be surprising!

Variation: **Each** player adds to the story with one sentence until the 10 sentences are completed.

LINES AND CIRCLES

No. of Players: unlimited
Age: 8 to adult
Supplies: paper and pencil for each player
Location: anywhere

One player thinks of an object he or she has seen on the trip and describes it for the other players to draw. The "catch" to this game is that the person describing the object may only use lines and circles in the description.

For example, the description of a fence might be "Make one line going from one end of the paper to the other, right to left. Make the line straight. Now make lines cross that line several inches apart going close from the top to the bottom of the page."

The result should be a fence or other object the player has described, but often what shows up on the page is hilariously different.

NAME A COLOR

No. of Players: unlimited
Age: all
Supplies: paper and pencil for each player
Location: anywhere

The players take turns naming colors and the others must draw something that is mainly of that color.

For example, a player who hears "red" might draw a fire engine, a stop sign or an apple.

I DREW THAT?

No. of Players: unlimited
Age: all
Supplies: a magazine and a piece of paper for each player
Location: anywhere

Put a magazine on top of each person's head and a piece of paper on top of the magazine. Everyone draws the same object or subject without looking at the paper. The results can be very funny.

PUPPETS

No. of Players: unlimited
Age: all
Supplies: a paper bag and pencil or crayon for each player
Location: anywhere

Take a small paper bag and turn it upside down. Draw eyes, a nose, a mouth and hair on the bag. Players place  their hands inside the bags to create puppets. Stuff the bag with crumpled newspaper for better control by smaller hands.

LEAF PRINTS

No. of Players: unlimited
Age: all
Supplies: a leaf and a piece of cardboard and paper for each player
Location: anywhere

Put any leaf on a piece of cardboard, vein side up. Then place a piece of paper on top of the leaf and color or shade with a pencil over the paper. The leaf outlines will come through as you color.

MY FAVORITE PLACE

No. of Players: unlimited
Age: all
Supplies: paper and pencil for each player
Location: anywhere

Players draw or color their favorite places or scenes encountered on the trip.

Variation: Draw the favorite place visited each day.

SPOON PUPPETS

No. of Players: unlimited
Age: all
Supplies: one spoon and a crayon for each player
Location: anywhere

Draw puppet faces on the back of plastic spoons and act out a favorite fairy tale or story.

WHAT I LOOKED LIKE ON VACATION

No. of Players: three
Age: all
Supplies: a flashlight and paper
Location: a motel room

After the family is settled down at night in the motel room, have one person stand sideways **close** to a wall. Shine a flashlight on the person's profile to create a shadow on the wall. Another person puts a piece of paper on the wall where the shadow appears and traces the face.

DESCRIPTIVE PICTURES

No. of Players: unlimited
Age: all
Supplies: paper and pencil for each player
Location: anywhere

One person draws a picture of any scene without the others looking. The same person now **describes** the picture and the others must try to duplicate the same scene on their own pieces of paper without seeing the original.

TRAVEL LOG

No. of Players: unlimited
Age: all
Supplies: paper and pencil for each player
Location: anywhere

Take a piece of paper and write at the top what was seen each day. Below that, draw a picture of the most interesting experience.

DOT TO DOT

No. of Players: two
Age: all
Supplies: one piece of paper and a pencil
Location: anywhere

Draw a picture or scene with dots at least one-half inch apart. Number the dots so a line can be drawn from dot to dot to make the picture. Now have another player connect the dots to complete the picture.

MARSHMALLOW SCULPTURE

No. of Players:	up to four
Age:	all
Supplies:	a bag of marshmallows, raisins and a box of toothpicks
Location:	anywhere

Put 20 or 30 marshmallows in a shallow box along with several small boxes of raisins and a box of toothpicks. Players create sculptures of people, places and things using the ingredients.

ART GAMES

FAMILY TREE

No. of Players: unlimited
Age: all
Supplies: paper and pencil for each player
Location: anywhere

Draw a tree with large branches on a piece of paper. Write down all the family members from both sides, including grandparents, parents, aunts, uncles and cousins.

The oldest members are placed in the top branches and the youngest in the bottom. The mother's side can be written on the left, the father's on the right.

GOOFY PICTURES

No. of Players: two or three
Age: all
Supplies: one piece of paper and a pencil
Location: anywhere

Fold a piece of paper into three equal pieces. With no one else looking, the first person draws the head of a human or animal on the first one-third of the paper, with the neck going slightly onto the second one-third of the paper. The head drawing should now be folded under so no one can see it.

The next person draws the body of a human or animal on the second one-third of the paper. The creature's

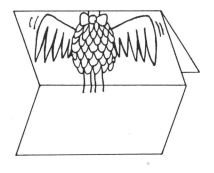

legs should extend slightly onto the last one-third of the paper. No one should see this drawing, either, and it should be folded under when finished.

The last person now draws legs on the last one-third of the paper without looking at the other drawings. When the picture is finished, it is opened up for all to see. The results should produce a goofy drawing and a good laugh.

TEAR A FACE

No. of Players: unlimited
Age: all
Supplies: a piece of newspaper for each player
Location: anywhere

Take turns creating each other's profiles by tearing the paper.

Variation: Tear profiles of the other person's entire body.

GUESSING GAMES —
Names and Objects

I SAW THAT!

No. of Players: unlimited
Age: all
Supplies: none
Location: anywhere

In ten words or less, everybody takes turns describing a television show or movie everyone has seen. The other players try to guess the title.

...AND THEN, THE PRINCE KISSES THE PRINCESS, AN'...

Scoring: Players receive one point for each correct guess. The first player to get 10 points wins.

Variation: One person describes a scene and the others try to guess the place, town, restaurant, etc.

TAP OUT

No. of Players:	four or more
Age:	8 to adult
Supplies:	small pieces of paper and a watch or clock
Location:	anywhere

This game has a time limit of one hour, but can be played while other games are under way.

Take as many small pieces of paper as there are players and mark one with an "X." Fold up the pieces of paper and let each player choose one. The player with the "X" is **It**, but tells **no** one. The person who is **It** then tries to eliminate the other players one by one by indicating to each using a signal everyone has agreed upon, such as a tap on the shoulder.

Meanwhile, each player has one chance to guess who **It** is, but must do so before being eliminated. If a person guesses correctly, the game starts over. If the guess is wrong, that player is out and the game continues.

FILL IN THE BLANK

No. of Players:	unlimited
Age:	all
Supplies:	none
Location:	anywhere

One player says a sentence but leaves out a key word. The others try to guess that word. For example, "I went shopping and bought a _____."

After each guess, a new clue is given in another sentence with that word still left out. So the next clue might be, "This _____ is found in a grocery store."

The next clue might be, "The _____ I bought is yellow."

Then someone might guess "banana" and win that round.

Up to 10 clues (sentences) can be given before someone else takes a turn.

Scoring: One point for each correct guess. Five points wins the game.

I SPY

No. of Players: unlimited
Age: all
Supplies: none
Location: anywhere

One player says, "I spy something red." The other players then take turns guessing what the object might be.

Variation: Instead of colors, use dimensions such as tall, flat, round, thin, wide, etc.

FIVE KEY WORDS

No. of Players: unlimited
Age: 8 to adult
Supplies: none
Location: anywhere

One player thinks of something that is animal, mineral or plant. Five words are given to the other players, who try to guess the object.

For example, the player is thinking "sun." Clue words could be "round," "bright," "sky," "hot," "day."

If no one guesses correctly, the word is given and another player starts over with a new word.

Variation: Give only three clues.

FIVE QUESTIONS

No. of Players:	unlimited
Age:	all
Supplies:	none
Location:	anywhere

One player picks an object that he or she has seen the same day. The other players take turns asking one question at a time about the object. The player who picked the object can only say "Yes" or "No" to each question.

After each player has taken three turns, each one guesses what the object might be. The players can have the same answers.

Scoring: Each correct guess earns one point. Five points wins the game.

FAMOUS CONVERSATIONS

No. of Players:	three or more
Age:	8 to adult
Supplies:	none
Location:	anywhere

Two players agree on a famous person but do not tell the other players. The same two players begin conversing about the famous person. Anytime during the conversation, the other players try to guess who it is. For example, if the famous person is Abraham Lincoln, one player might say, "This person lived about a hundred years ago." The other player might say, "Yes, and he lived when there was a huge war."

The conversation continues until someone guesses the famous person.

GUESSING GAMES —
Time and Distance

TIME'S UP

No. of Players:	unlimited
Age:	all
Supplies:	a watch with a second hand
Location:	anywhere

One player uses the watch to time one minute and begins by saying "go" at the beginning of the minute. The other players cannot see the watch, but may say "Stop" at the moment they believe a minute is up.

Scoring: The player who gets closest to a minute without exceeding the time limit wins.

CAR COLORS

No. of Players:	unlimited
Age:	all
Supplies:	none
Location:	a view of other cars

Before the next car (or any vehicle) comes into view, each person guesses what color it will be. Players are allowed to guess the same color.

Scoring: One point is awarded for each correct guess. Ten points wins the game.

Variations: Try to guess the kind of car that will pass from the opposite direction. You could try to guess the make; two-door or four-door; a truck, bus or car.

WHAT TIME IS IT?

No. of Players: unlimited
Age: all
Supplies: a watch or clock
Location: anywhere

On long trips, restless passengers often ask the time. In this game, **no one** can ask the time. Every so often, though, a leader, who is the only one who can see the watch or clock, can ask the others, "What time is it?"

Scoring: The player closes to the correct time gets one point. Five points wins the game.

Variation: If the leader chooses to let the players ask the time, they must all guess and the closest guess wins (same scoring). No one can ask more than once an hour, or no time is given.

WHERE WAS THAT PLACE?

No. of Players: unlimited
Age: all
Supplies: a map of the area you've traveled through
Location: in a car or train

After traveling at least 500 miles, give a chosen leader the map. The leader picks two towns that the family has traveled through. Each person guesses which town was traveled through first.

Scoring: One point for each correct guess. Ten points wins.

PEOPLE POINTS

No. of Players: unlimited
Age: all
Supplies: none
Location: a view of other cars

Before the next car from the opposite direction comes into view, each person guesses out loud how many people will be in it.

Scoring: Players get one point for each correct guess. Ten points wins the game.

FILL UP

No. of Players: unlimited
Age: all
Supplies: none
Location: in a car

After gassing up the auto, the players guess how many miles it will be to the next fill up.

Scoring: The closest guess wins.

PERFECT PLACEMENT

No. of Players:	three
Age:	all
Supplies:	three sets of the same objects and three magazines or pieces of cardboard
Location:	anywhere

The players place an identical number of the same objects on their magazines or pieces of cardboard.

They then chose one player to begin. Without allowing the other players to see, that player arranges all the objects in a certain pattern on the board, and describes the arrangement to the other players.

The other player who most closely arranges the objects like the first player's wins the round.

The players take turns arranging and describing their objects.

IMAGINATION GAMES

CLOUDY DAY GAME

No. of Players: unlimited
Age: all
Supplies: none
Location: in a car or train on a cloudy day

Each person takes a turn at picking a cloud and the rest try to find a face or animal in that cloud.

Variation: One person says, "I see [an object] in that cloud," and everyone else tries to guess which cloud the person has in mind.

TELL ME A STORY

No. of Players: unlimited
Age: all
Supplies: a watch or clock
Location: in a car or train

Each person picks an object that he or she can see or has seen over a certain period of time and another player has one minute to think up a story about the object. During the next minute the second person must tell a story **nonstop**. The story should have a situation, some characters with names and descriptions and a final outcome.

For example, the object could be an old house. After thinking for one minute, the player would tell a story about how there once was a little girl named Isabel who had long red hair and big brown freckles who wanted her own house and so she began going to construction sites and asking the workers for pieces and bits until she had enough pieces and bits to build her own house, and how she built that house and lived in it until the day she died, and then how her children lived in it and her grandchildren live in it today, etc., etc.

Other good objects might be a dog in a yard, a dirt road, an old car or people passing in another vehicle.

Scoring: Players win points by telling complete stories for the entire minute. Five points wins the game.

SUNSET TIME

No. of Players:	unlimited
Age:	all
Supplies:	none
Location:	where you can see the sun just after setting

Everyone takes turns trying to name as many colors in the sky as possible after the sun sets. Avoid playing this until the sun is out of view to prevent eye damage.

Variations: Name the colors on a mountain, hillside, desert or outside anywhere.

WHICH WOULD YOU BE

No. of Players: unlimited
Age: all
Supplies: none
Location: anywhere

Everyone takes turns asking players which of two living or nonliving things they'd like to be and why. They must choose one and answer promptly.

For example, "Which would you rather be, a hammer or a nail?" The person might reply, "A hammer because I could pound on stuff."

There are no right or wrong answers.

LOTTERY WINNER

No. of Players: unlimited
Age: all
Supplies: none
Location: anywhere

Players take turns pretending they've won a million dollars and describing how all the money will be spent.

COUPONS

No. of Players: unlimited
Age: all
Supplies: paper and pencil for each player
Location: anywhere

Using the paper and pencil, each person creates two coupons that describe two nice things the creator will do for someone else while on the trip.
For example: "I, Nicole Smith, promise to let my brother shower first for three nights."

MAGAZINE GAMES

ALPHABET PICTURES

No. of Players: unlimited
Age: all
Supplies: a magazine and a pencil for each player
Location: anywhere

Have a contest to see who can find the most pictures in a magazine that start with each letter of the alphabet.

For example, for the letter "H" someone could find a house, a hat, a horse, a handle, etc.

Circle the letters or write down the item and page number so the magazines can be used again.

MAKE OVERS

No. of Players: unlimited
Age: all
Supplies: a discarded magazine for each player, pencils, pens or crayons
Location: anywhere

Use crayons, pens and pencils to make people in magazines look silly. Mustaches, black teeth, crazy hats and colorful clothes can make funny pictures.

MAGAZINE FRENZY

No. of Players: unlimited
Age: 7 to adult
Supplies: a discarded magazine and a watch or clock
Location: anywhere

Have someone who isn't playing tear out 10 or more pages. The pages are then all placed back in the magazine upside down, in the wrong order or backward.

Time players to see how fast they can correct the order.

Scoring: The person with the fastest time wins.

MIXED UP PEOPLE

No. of Players: two
Age: all
Supplies: a discarded magazine and a watch or clock
Location: anywhere

Take three pictures of people out of a discarded magazine. Carefully tear each picture into three pieces and mix them up. Give them to another player and time the person to see how quickly he or she can put the pictures back together.

FAN LETTER

No. of Players: unlimited
Age: 7 to adult
Supplies: paper and pencil or pen for each player
Location: anywhere

Each person picks a favorite television or movie star from a magazine and writes a letter to that person. Upon return home or arrival in a city large enough to have a local television station, call the station that airs the show and find out where to send the fan letter.

74

MUSIC AND SOUND
GAMES

SING IT OUT

No. of Players:	unlimited
Age:	all
Supplies:	none
Location:	anywhere

The first player sings the entire song *Twinkle, Twinkle, Little Star*. The next player also sings the entire song but leaves out the last word. The third player repeats the song but leaves out the last word and the second-to-last word.

The song continues around to the players until all of the words have been left out. Any player who sings the song incorrectly must try again until successful.

Variation: Leave out the song's first word, then the first and second word, etc.

GOOD LUNGS

No. of Players: unlimited
Age: all
Supplies: a watch or clock
Location: anywhere

On the word "go," everyone begins to whistle. The person who whistles the longest with one breath of air wins the round.

Scoring: After several rounds, the person with the longest time is the champ.

HUM A TUNE

No. of Players:	unlimited
Age:	7 to adult
Supplies:	none
Location:	anywhere

Each person takes a turn humming a tune and the other players try to guess the tune's title. The category of the tunes can be announced each round. For example, your categories might be movie themes, television show themes, top forty tunes or commercial tunes.

ADD A BAR

No. of Players: unlimited
Age: 7 to adult
Supplies: none
Location: anywhere

One person sings or hums a few bars of a song and the next player must add the next bar. Each player in turn hums or sings an additional bar until the song is finished.

SOUND EFFECTS

No. of Players: unlimited
Age: all
Supplies: none
Location: anywhere

Each player takes a turn naming an object that makes a sound and the rest of the players imitate the sound. The results can be very funny.

Some examples:

- ◆ truck putting on the brakes
- ◆ an ocean in a storm
- ◆ barnyard sounds
- ◆ birds flying
- ◆ a person taking a fast food order.

SINGING CONVERSATION

No. of Players: unlimited
Age: all
Supplies: a watch or clock (optional)
Location: anywhere

Pick a well-known tune such as *Mary Had a Little Lamb*. Everyone must now **sing** their conversations to the tune of *Mary Had a Little Lamb*. Set a time or distance limit.

ROADSIDE PARK STOP

When you're driving, roadside parks offer lots of fun! Here are some of the things you can do when you stop to take a rest:

◆ Each person picks up an object from the roadside stop, such as a flower, rock, twig or leaf. (Please make sure the object is something you are allowed to take, though!) Once everyone is back in the car, each person draws a picture of the object picked up at the stop.

◆ Passengers can collect a different rock, leaf or twig at each stop, and start a collection. (Once again, be sure it is legal to remove these objects.)

After you're back on the road:

◆ Each person remembers or writes down two or three objects seen at the roadside stop. The others can take turns guessing the objects.

◆ It's fun, too, to keep a log of the different kinds of birds, trees, flowers, cars, etc. seen on the trip.

NUMBER AND STRATEGY GAMES

THE NUMBER PICTURE

No. of Players: unlimited
Age: 7 to adult
Supplies: paper and pencil for each player
Location: anywhere

A leader calls out a number and the players must draw a picture using the number.

For example, if the leader calls out, "Two!" the picture might look like this:

TRAVELING MATH

No. of Players: unlimited
Age: 8 to adult
Supplies: paper and pencil for each player and a map of the area you
are traveling through
Location: car

The players add the red mileage numbers on the map from city to city as they are traveling through each place.

MATCHING NUMBERS

No. of Players: unlimited
Age: all
Supplies: paper and pencil for each player
Location: anywhere

Everyone writes the numbers one through 10 all over their paper. Next they write the numbers on the paper again, but in different places away from the first set of numbers.

Players then exchange papers and see who can match up the numbers first by connecting them with lines.

Scoring: The first player to match all the numbers is the winner.

Variation: Play the game as usual, but the connecting lines cannot cross each other.

HIGHER, LOWER

No. of Players: unlimited
Age: 7 to adult
Supplies: none
Location: anywhere

A leader picks a number between one and 1,000 but tells no one. Each player in turn then tries to guess the number.

The leader can only respond by answering "higher" if the guess is larger than the number, or "lower" if the guess is smaller. The player who finally guesses the number becomes the next leader.

BINGO

No. of Players:	unlimited
Age:	all
Supplies:	a homemade bingo card (see next page) and pencil for each player, a piece of paper that can be torn into 100 pieces, a bag or other container to use as a shaker
Location:	anywhere

Tear a piece of paper into 100 pieces. Number the pieces from one to 100. Place the numbered pieces in a bag or container and shake them up.

One person is picked as the caller.

The other players make their own cards by copying the diagram on the next page. Players then pick the designated numbers and place them on their card (see diagram).

The caller begins by pulling out a piece of paper and calling the number on it. If it matches a player's card, that player puts an "X" through the box containing the same number.

Scoring: The first player to "X" out five boxes horizontally, vertically or diagonally wins.

Variation: The person to fill all the boxes wins.

		FREE SPOT		

pick any numbers between 1–20 and place in boxes

pick any numbers between 21–40 and place in boxes

pick any numbers between 41–60 and place in boxes

pick any numbers between 61–80 and place in boxes

pick any numbers between 81–100 and place in boxes

GROCERY MATH

No. of Players: unlimited
Age: all
Supplies: paper and pencil for each player
Location: on the road

Have an adult make a list of five to 10 items someone might purchase at the store while on the trip. Everyone copies the same list, writes their guess of each item's cost, then adds up the amounts.

Scoring: At the store, the costs can be checked and the closest total wins.

BEEP

No. of Players:	unlimited
Age:	8 to adult
Supplies:	none
Location:	anywhere

In this game the word "beep" is said instead of "five" and any number that is a multiple of five (for example, 10, 15, 20, etc.).

The first person starts the game by saying the number one. The second person says the number two and so on until the number five comes up. At "five," the person says, "Beep."

If any person says the number instead of "beep," that person is out of the game.

Scoring: The last person left wins.

Variation: Use any number and its multiples in place of five. (For example, players say "beep" on the number three and multiples of three: "One." "Two." "Beep." "Four." "Five." "Beep." etc.)

LICENSE COMBINATIONS

No. of Players: unlimited
Age: all
Supplies: none
Location: on the road

Each player picks any two numbers, one through nine. All the players then begin searching for a license plate containing those two numbers.

Scoring: The first player who succeeds wins.

Variation: Players have to find license plates with the two numbers together.

BOXES

No. of Players:	unlimited
Age:	7 to adult
Supplies:	one piece of paper and a pencil
Location:	anywhere

Copy the dot pattern on the next page. Using it, players take turns making a line from one dot to any other closest dot, just like the example shown on this page.

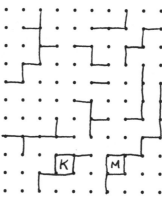

Each player tries to add the fourth line to three others to create a box, and then puts his or her initials inside each completed box.

Scoring: The player with the most completed boxes wins.

Use this pattern for the Boxes game and Line Trap game.

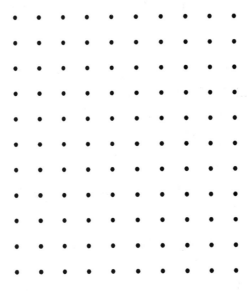

LINE TRAP

No. of Players: two
Age: 7 to adult
Supplies: one piece of paper and a pencil
Location: anywhere

Copy the dots on the previous page. The first player draws a line from one dot to any other closest dot. The second player must draw a line that extends from the first player's line to another closest dot. A dot can only have a line drawn from it once.

Each player tries to force the other back to a dot that already has a line drawn to it.

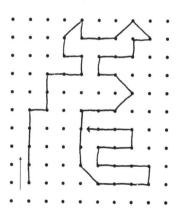

THREE IN A ROW

No. of Players: two
Age: 7 to adult
Supplies: five pennies (or any coin) and five dimes (or any coin)
Location: anywhere

Draw the diagram shown here. Each player takes five similar coins (if there are 10 of the same coin, you can use heads as one set and tails as the other).

The first player places a coin on any dot. The second player does the same, and the two then take turns. Coins cannot be placed on top of other coins.

Scoring: The first player to have three coins horizontally, vertically or diagonally wins.

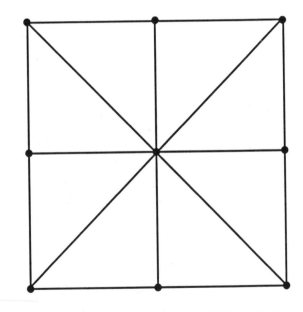

SEARCHING GAMES

WHO SAW THE MOST?

No. of Players: unlimited
Age: 7 to adult
Supplies: none
Location: on the road or train

One person starts the game by saying, "I saw one [item] on the trip."

For example, "I saw one **cloud** on the trip." It does not matter if there are dozens of clouds to see as long as there is at least one.

The next person says, "I saw two [items] on the trip," naming anything of which the player has seen at **least** two objects. The game progresses numerically and players drop out if they fail to name an object when it's their turn.

Another example might be, "I saw 76 tires on the trip." No objects may be repeated and, in the case of something like tires, the person must have seen at **least** 76 tires.

FIND IT FAST

No. of Players: unlimited

Age: all

Supplies: a bag you can not see through, 20 small objects and a watch with a second hand

Location: anywhere

Put 20 small objects in the bag. Have one player reach in without looking and pull out any item.

The object is then placed back in the bag and the bag is shaken to mix up the contents. The same player reaches in without looking and tries to find and retrieve the object as fast as possible.

Each player takes a turn and is timed.

Scoring: The fastest time wins.

STATE PLATES

No. of Players: unlimited
Age: all
Supplies: one piece of paper and a pencil
Location: on the road

Write down the license plates of different states as you see them on the trip.

Scoring: The person who finds the most states wins.

ROAD MAP

No. of Players: unlimited
Age: 7 to adult
Supplies: a map of the area you are traveling through
Location: on the road

One person picks a town on the road map and the players have one minute to find the place.

The person who picks the place must set up reasonable boundaries by saying, for example, "The town is between Mainville and Elmwood." The towns should also be no farther than 100 to 200 miles apart.

Variation: Use any map.

I'M OUT THERE SOMEWHERE

No. of Players:	unlimited
Age:	7 to adult
Supplies:	none
Location:	in a car or train

The players try to find something outside the car that starts with each letter of one of the player's names.

For example, if the name chosen is Jenny:

J	Jeep
e	earth
n	newspaper
n	nail
y	yard.

Letters on signs, etc., do not count, and the items do not have to be in the same order as they fall in the player's name.

Scoring: The first person to name all the objects is the winner.

Variation: The objects must be found in the same order as the letters in the person's name.

CHECK IT OFF

No. of Players: unlimited
Age: all
Supplies: paper and pencil for each player
Location: in a car or train

An adult should make a list of common and uncommon objects that might be seen on the journey. Each player receives an identical list and checks off the items as they are spotted. Some things that might be on the list are a barn with a red roof, a blue four-door car, three cows standing in a field, a town with a McDonald's restaurant.

Scoring: The first one who completes the list wins.

MY CAR

No. of Players: unlimited
Age: all
Supplies: none
Location: on the road

The players pick makes of cars or trucks they wish to search for. Each player should have a different make and must inform all the other players what has been chosen. When a player's vehicle is seen, he or she says, "My car."

Scoring: Ten "my cars" wins the game.

Variation: Colors may be substituted for make of vehicle.

WORD GAMES — Verbal

WHO CAN NAME THE MOST?

No. of Players: unlimited
Age: 10 to adult
Supplies: none
Location: anywhere

One player starts by naming a state. The next player must name a different state and the contest rotates to each player until one person is stumped. Repeats are not allowed and each person gets 10 seconds to answer.

Variations: Name different cars, movie stars, singers, television shows, objects in a kitchen or living room, types of stores, colors, trees or flowers.

EARTH, WATER, AIR

No. of Players: unlimited
Age: 8 to adult
Supplies: none
Location: anywhere

The players take turns saying "earth," "water" or "air." They then point to or touch a player who has five seconds to name something that inhabits one of those places. The thing does not have to be alive.

For example, one player might say, "Air!" and touch another player. The second player replies, "Robin."

Scoring: Players can keep score of one point for each correct guess. Ten points wins the game.

SILLY QUESTIONS

No. of Players: unlimited
Age: all
Supplies: none
Location: anywhere

One player invents a silly phrase that each player must say after any question is asked.

For example, the first player might pick the phrase "only when I sneeze." Then the first player asks another, "Have you been to Florida?" The second player answers, "Only when I sneeze."

This game is a lot of silly fun.

ADD A PHRASE

No. of Players: unlimited
Age: 7 to adult
Supplies: none
Location: anywhere

One person starts the game by saying any three-word phrase he or she can think of. The next person must say the first phrase, then add another three-word phrase. Each player must say all of the previous phrases and then add another. The story goes on until any person forgets to repeat all of the phrases in order. When this happens, that player is out until the next game.

For example, the first player might say, "Two big dogs." Then the second might say, "Two big dogs" (the first phrase) "walked toward me" (the second phrase). The third player might say, "Two big dogs walked toward me, wagging their tails." The fourth player might say, "Two big dogs walked toward me, wagging their tails very, very fast."

Scoring: Players receive one point for each successful turn with at **least** four phrases. The example above would be worth one point.

Variations: The words can be increased to any number.

WHAT'S ON YOUR MIND?

No. of Players: unlimited
Age: all
Supplies: none
Location: anywhere

One player starts by saying the first word that comes into his or her mind. The next player **responds** to the word by saying the first word that comes into his or her mind.

This continues with players saying the first words that come into their minds.

Each player must answer immediately and the game should continue for one minute.

The words spoken are often amusing and interesting.

RHYME WITH MY MIND

No. of Players: unlimited
Age: 8 to adult
Supplies: none
Location: anywhere

One player thinks of a word and tells the other players another word that rhymes with the chosen secret word.

The other players now take turns trying to guess the secret word. If a player guesses the word, that player gets to choose a new secret word.

For example, if the word the player is thinking of is "tree," he or she might say aloud, "Knee." The other players might guess "bee" "pea," "free" until someone finally calls out the answer: "Tree!" The person who said "tree" chooses the next secret word.

LICENSE TO SPELL

No. of Players: unlimited
Age: all
Supplies: none
Location: in a car

Try to find and spell the letters of the state you are traveling through in the large letters of license plates as they pass by.

Variations: Find and spell any simple word, or find and spell the letters of the state or any chosen word in **order**.

PASS WORD

No. of Players:	unlimited
Age:	8 to adult
Supplies:	one piece of paper and a pencil
Location:	anywhere

One person is chosen as Master of Ceremonies. The MC writes a word on a small piece of paper, which is hidden from the players. The MC then gives the players clues.

The players try to guess the word.

For example, the word is "house." The MC gives the clue "building." One player guesses, "High-rise." Another guesses, "School," and so on until someone finally says, "House."

Scoring: The player who guesses right first wins.

YES AND NO

No. of Players: unlimited
Age: all
Supplies: none
Location: anywhere

The responses "yes" and "no" cannot be used in conversation for 30 minutes.

The fun begins when everyone tries to trick the other players while at the same time avoiding saying "yes" and "no" themselves.

YOU WANT TO DRIVE AWHILE?

INITIAL ANSWERS

No. of Players: unlimited
Age: 8 to adult
Supplies: none
Location: anywhere

Each player is asked questions by a leader. All must answer with the initials of their names.

For example, when Paul Smith is asked, "What is your favorite sport?" he might answer, "Playing soccer."

Scoring: Score one point for answering with the correct response. Twenty points wins the game.

STATE SENTENCE

No. of Players: unlimited
Age: 8 to adult
Supplies: none
Location: anywhere

Someone picks the name of a state or town and the other players must make a sentence out of the letters in the state or town chosen.

For instance, if the place chosen is Maine, the sentence might be "<u>M</u>y <u>a</u>unt <u>i</u>s <u>n</u>ow <u>e</u>xcited."

WORD GAMES —
Paper and Pencil

TOWER

No. of Players: unlimited
Age: 9 to adult
Supplies: paper and pencil for each player
Location: anywhere

Write any letter on a piece of paper. Now repeat the letter down the page, adding new letters to the **first** letter each time to form a new word. As you go down the page, add one more letter for each level.
For example:

> G
>
> Go
>
> Gas
>
> Game
>
> Games
>
> Gamble.

VACATION

No. of Players: unlimited
Age: 10 to adult
Supplies: paper and pencil for each player
Location: anywhere

Find and write down as many words as you can from the word "vacation."

Variations: Use other words such as:

- "traveling"
- "suitcase"
- "swimming pool"
- "automobile"
- The name of the state you're traveling through.

UNSCRAMBLE

No. of Players:	unlimited
Age:	9 to adult
Supplies:	paper and pencil for each player and a watch or clock
Location:	anywhere

Have someone write 10 names of objects everyone has seen on the trip. No one is to see this list. On another piece of paper have the same person scramble the letters in the words. For example, "road" might become "**dora**."

The second piece of paper is given to the other players. They then try to unscramble the words on their own piece of paper.

Scoring: The player who unscrambles all the words fastest wins.

Variations: Set a time limit, and the player who unscrambles the most in that period of time wins. Or you can announce and use categories for the scrambled words. Some examples are types of dogs or other animals, types of cars, states, types of trees, types of flowers, colors, types of clothing.

HANGMAN

No. of Players: unlimited
Age: 8 to adult
Supplies: one piece of paper and a pencil
Location: anywhere

One player draws a hangman stand.
That player then thinks of a word and
draws lines for each letter below the stand.

Another player then guesses a letter. If
that person guesses one of the letters
that appears in the word, the first player
fills in the space or spaces where it
belongs.

_ _ E E _ A _

If the guess is incorrect, the first player draws a person's head.
The other players now take turns guessing other letters. If the guesses are correct, the first player fills in the letters on the lines beneath the stand. If the guesses are incorrect, the first player adds another part to the person hanging from the stand. (The body can include eyes, ears, etc.)

The game continues until the players guess the word or the person's body is complete.

If a player guesses the word, that person gets to choose the next word. If the body is completed before the word is guessed, the first player gets to choose another word, and the game starts over.

F R E E W A Y

WORD GAMES — Paper and Pencil

TOWER OF NAMES

No. of Players: unlimited
Age: all
Supplies: paper and a pencil for each player
Location: anywhere

All the players write the same name of a town or state on their own piece of paper, doubling the second letter, tripling the third letter, etc.:

T

ee

xxx

aaaa

sssss.

One player starts the game by writing down one of the letters on another part of his or her piece of paper that the others cannot see.

Now the other players guess out loud which letter they think was written. After all the players have guessed, the letter is revealed. Any player who guessed correctly can cross off one of those letters on his or her piece of paper.

All the players take turns writing down a letter.

Scoring: The first player to cross off all the letters in the name is the winner.

THERE'S A RELATIONSHIP

No. of Players: unlimited
Age: 9 to adult
Supplies: paper and pencil for each player and a watch or clock
Location: anywhere

One player choses a subject. On the word "go," everyone writes down as many words as they can think of about a particular subject. Good subjects might be ocean, city, desert, house, trees, etc.

For example, if the subject is mountain, the players could write "trail," "hike," "birds."

Scoring: The player who writes down the most words related to the subject within a set time limit wins.

SEE AND SPELL

No. of Players: unlimited
Age: 8 to adult
Supplies: paper and pencil for each player
Location: anywhere

An adult may want to be the judge in this game. One player calls out loud an object that he or she sees. All the other players write down the word. Every correct spelling earns one point.

Each player takes turns picking objects.

Scoring: Ten points wins the game.

WHAT'S IN A NAME?

No. of Players: unlimited
Age: 9 to adult
Supplies: paper and pencil for each player
Location: anywhere

Everyone prints one player's full name on their paper. Within five minutes, everyone tries to make as many words as possible out of the letters in the entire name.

For example, everyone writes down "Jane Smith."

One player comes up with "it," "mite," "ant," "sat," "hat."

Scoring: Players receive one point for each word made. Twenty points wins the game.

ABOUT THE AUTHOR

Marie Boatness received her bachelor of science degree from Northwest Missouri State University and master of science degree in Physical Education from Arizona State University. For the past 20 years, she has been teaching physical education to children of all ages. This experience and involvement has given Marie a broad understanding of the types of activities children enjoy.

While traveling throughout the United States and Canada, the Boatness family tested and developed the ideas and games that have become *Travel Games For The Family*.

GAME INDEX

TRAVEL GAMES FOR THE FAMILY

...is the perfect antidote for the on-the-road fidgets! There are games for every age and every interest that will make the hours melt away! You'll want a copy available for everything from that holiday trip to Grandma's to the crosstown ride to the mall, so order yours today!

Please send me _____ copies of *Travel Games For The Family* at $9.95 each; plus $2 per book for postage and handling (Arizona residents add 67¢ tax per book). Allow three weeks for delivery.

Name _____

Address _____

City _____ State_____ Zip _____

My check or money order payable to Canyon Creek Press, in the amount of $_____, is enclosed.

Mail to: Canyon Creek Press
5714 E. Dale Lane
Cave Creek Arizona 85331

WHAT GAMES DO YOU PLAY?

Every family and group has its own favorite games. Would you like to share one—or a variation of one of those in this book—with other people? Please fill out the front and back of this form and mail it to us at Canyon Creek Press, 5714 E. Dale Lane, Cave Creek AZ 85331. If we select your game, we'll write you—and send you a copy of the book! Thank you!

✂ —

No. of Players: _____

Age: _____

Supplies: _____

Location: _____

Directions: _____

_____

_____

_____

_____

_____

_____

_____

_____

_____

Variation:_____

Scoring: _____

- -

Your Name _____

Your Address_____

Your City, State and Zip Code _____

Your Phone Number _____

Your Age _____

Your School_____

Thank You!

794   BOA   73-97

Boatness
TRAVEL GAMES FOR THE FAMILY

DATE DUE